Pretty Melanin Me!

Markita Richards

Illustrations by Blueberry Illustrations

To my amazing husband, Neil thank you for believing in my vision and me always. To my babies Jadon, Janiyah, and Jayla you are my inspiration and this is for y'all.

My mommy Teresa thank you for the encouragement and love you have always given me. To my baby sister, Makenzie thank you for the support and listening during this process. My auntie Angel thank you for always telling me how pretty I was as a child.

This book is in loving memory of my courageous Grandmama Azzie Lee Williams you are truly missed.

Xoxo,
M.L.R.

Mommy mommy mommy!!
Yes Jade!
That's Alley, she is in my class.
Mommy, why is my skin darker than Alley's?

Jade because you have, more melanin than her!
What's MELON Mommy!!??

MELANIN is the pigmentation of your beautiful skin!
You have a beautiful cocoa caramel
tone that's smooth and soft.

Your beautiful complexion can match any dress you would like to wear no matter the color of cloth.

Jade you are so gorgeous when the sun kisses your skin it flourishes into a brown sugar honey golden glow.

From your black curly, wavy, kinky hair,
to your beautiful brown eyes,
your button nose, and even
your pretty melanin toes.

You are Uniquely YOU!

You are perfectly dipped in chocolate, making you a Melanin princess. No matter the color of your skin, you can be anything you DREAM.

Could I be A Doctor,
A Lawyer, A Ballerina,
A Firefighter,
A Policewoman,
Even an Astronaut?

SURE, YOU CAN!

You come from a lineage of
different shades of brown.
No matter the shade of your skin,
your beauty come from within.

Repeat after me the color of my skin will not define me, when I grow up, I can be anything I want to BE!

You are not just beautiful to be a brown girl you are beautiful because you are beautiful.

You are Be-YOU-Tiful

You are PERFECT in the skin you are in!

Jade look in the
mirror and tell me
who do you see!

Mommy, I see
Pretty Melanin Me!

Markita Richards is a wife, a mother of three, daughter, sister, aunt, self-awareness coach, and advocate. Pretty Melanin Me has been produced to help promote self-esteem, self-confidence, and self-love in little girls of color. Markita holds a degree in Psychology and believes in educating little girls on the importance of loving themselves from within. Pretty Melanin Me is her debut children's book and the introductory series of stories on building resilience in children. Markita believes that by instilling self-value in little girls at a young age, they will likely not feel objectified by social standards to look and be a certain way. Pretty Melanin Me is a story about how beautiful Melanin is. It is never too early to teach little girls the importance of self-love and self-awareness to steer from society's idealization of what pretty is and to break the pathology of colorism.

www.ingramcontent.com/pod-product-compliance
Lightning Source LLC
Chambersburg PA
CBHW042015090426

42811CB00015B/1651